DARK SHIP

THE CRUISE FROM HELL

ALEXANDER FLINT

outskirts press

TO THE YOUTH OF MY FAMILY,
ALEXA, ZOE, ADRIANA, SYDNEY,
ALAINA, AND ZANDER

TABLE OF CONTENTS

DARK SHIP

This was to be a world cruise to take me to parts of the world I had never visited. I looked forward to experiencing the Far East, Southeast Asia, India, and all exotic areas in between. After I booked passage, I anticipated the voyage for nearly a year.

I expected to see and photograph birds and wildlife in their natural habitat for my first time. This came true and was exciting for me. I photographed the white eagle hunting fish. I also saw a monitor lizard climbing a rock. There were bats and a mudskipper in Langkawi, Malaysia. Also, I found the giant fruit bats, also known as flying foxes, in a park in the middle of a city in Sri Lanka.

On our first stop in Hong Kong, I planned to buy a custom-tailored suit. I found a tailor quite easily. He actually found me. An agent in the street, recognizing me as a tourist, approached and led me to Pacific Fashions, International Bespoke Tailor, a Hong Kong government registered shop on 83-87 Nathan

Road in Hong Kong's Kowloon section. I was shown the fabrics, selected one I liked, measured, and the order was placed. I fretted over whether the suit would be ready, or if the shop would even be there when we returned two weeks later. It not only was ready, but it fit perfectly. I liked it so much I ordered another suit and shirt to be mailed to my home in Florida.

Job's Tomb in Oman was interesting. I never knew who Job was, but found out from the tour guide that he was a prophet who lived around 800 AD. In addition, he is important because all three major religions revere him as someone important. Christianity, Judaism, and Islam all acknowledge Job's significance. The tour guide also informed us that there are four tombs for Job scattered around the Middle East. I was shocked to find out he was not buried at this tomb in Oman. It was thought he was buried in Iraq, but Iran claims he is buried there. When I asked why there was a tomb for him here in Salalah, I was told that he lived here. I was shocked. I thought that a tomb is where a person is entombed, or placed.

The only tomb I am familiar with in the United States is Grant's Tomb, located on the Hudson River in New York. I am reasonably certain that Ulysses S. Grant is entombed there. Grant was the general who led the North to victory in the United States Civil War. There are no other locations where he is claimed to be buried.

I was also pleasantly moved by the Bedouin camp where we ate. The food and music were enjoyable. Camels were seen everywhere in Oman and Jordan. I learned that Bedouins do not always comply with laws of the Islamic state. In a country where women wear clothing that forces them to hide their feminine features, the Bedouin women ignore that government pressure. I photographed one who boldly showed her face and Western-world makeup.

Everything sounds great, right? Well, yes and no. I have been on a dozen luxury cruises and always enjoyed myself. Something was dreadfully wrong on this cruise. I am still trying to understand what it was.

During the times of the early sailing vessels, massive superstitions abounded. When a ship was believed to be cursed, it was called a *Phantom Ship* or a *Dark Ship*. With all that went wrong on this ship, it had to have been cursed. When you read all the matters written of here, the only explanation is that this luxury cruise ship—the one I took this world cruise on—is a cursed *Dark Ship*.

This book was written before the Coronavirus was identified. We visited several ports in China and throughout the Far East.

Could it be possible that the illness we suffered in the spring of 2019 was the beginning of the pandemic? Is it possible the two helicopter evacuations as sea were to remove sick Coronavirus victims?

Chapter 1

THE FLOATING PETRI DISH

Petri dishes are clear, round dishes that have an airtight cover with an organic jelly inside to provide food for microorganisms. They are used in medical laboratories for testing how bacteria grow, and what method laboratory scientists can use to combat threatening germs. I have heard this ship called a floating petri dish due to the apparent plethora of contaminants within her bulkheads and common areas.

I believe slack management and improper training of personnel are to blame. The dining room services, housekeeping, pursers' desk, medical center, tour office, and voyage sales department are all in need of drastic overhaul. Sometimes I think fixing these broken systems cannot be done.

I am convinced there also is something wrong with the design of the heating and air-conditioning system, because most guests seem to have a persistent cough. This has come to be known as the Cursed Cabin Cough. The widespread nature of this cough is most noticeable when one is seated in a quiet location where many people are gathered. When one is on a tour bus, in the theater, or on an elevator, the area is permeated with the sound of coughs. It seems that when one person coughs, there is an impulse magically transported to the cough reflexes of the rest of the group, which is responded to by other people who respond in kind.

I get a cold about once every three years. After eleven days on this ship, I came down with a severe upper respiratory infection—more like the flu than a cold. This was to be the first of three upper respiratory infections I suffered on this luxury world cruise. Thankfully I brought medication for just such an emergency. The old-fashioned Vicks VapoRub worked best for me. My father used to say if you treat a cold properly, it will last for seven days. If you ignore it, it will be gone in a week. Dad was never wrong, but thankfully he had never experienced this cursed ship.

March 7th, eight weeks later, I suffered another whopper of a cold. Both were replete with fever, deep cough, painful joints, photosensitivity, and two tissue boxes worth of a running nose. Ugh! It appeared my cabin steward was not used to monitoring the supplies in his rooms, so I had to constantly request more tissue boxes. Now I begin to analyze why. He was a nice man, but it seems that he was ill-trained, and his supervisors were nonexistent.

I noticed that whenever we entered the dining areas there were uniformed staff members at the entrance with bottles of hand sanitizer. They'd squirt a blob on your hands so anything you touch is not contaminated. The idea is right, but the minute you touch something else which is not sterile, you have germ-laden hands. So, what is the first item handed to you when you are seated at your dinner table? The menu! It is touched by every waiter and passenger before you. Your hands are now in need of another blob of cleaning goo, which is not available. Also, when you are initially seated, you always grab your heavy chair to adjust it. So, more contamination on your hands. I wonder, are the chairs and menus ever sanitized?

Are the food handlers ever checked for unsanitary hands or are their mouths and noses covered with surgical masks? A surgical mask on food handlers would protect the food by preventing breath or droplet spray from their mouths when they speak from landing on the food. I don't think those precautions were taken. The prevailing sickness and the pervasive cabin cough had to be coming from somewhere. I wonder if the cruise ship's management was as concerned as I was.

On the *Azamara Quest*, on which I enjoyed a two-week cruise in 2017, the captain recognized the transmission of infection through human contact. He requested that, instead of shaking hands with everyone you were introduced to, you do a fist bump instead. Performing this act as a social habit upon meeting someone ensures that the germ-laden areas of your palm, which is used to stifle coughs and sneezes, doesn't contact anyone else.

Let us consider the cabin we lived in.

The room steward cleans your room twice a day. He (or she) wears rubber gloves to protect himself from the germ-laden items he touches. This would include toilet, sink, and the bathroom floor. He wears the same gloves to clean your toilet and every other of the dozen or so cabins in his area of responsibility. Those gloves then touch your door handles, pillowcases, and TV remote. Furthermore, they are worn when putting the neat corner folds on your tissue boxes and toilet paper rolls. The contaminated tissues' next contact is often with your nostrils, eyes, or face. The room steward's hands are protected from the germs in all the cabins he services. His hands are protected, but everything he touches in each of his rooms is contaminated. I wonder if the managers ever tell the stewards to change or sanitize those gloves when leaving one cabin and entering another. I strongly doubt it. It makes me wonder if there are functional supervisors for the room stewards.

I made a request to have the air filter in my room changed. Like most requests made on the ship, this met with negative results. The room steward told me there are no air filters. I insisted there were and requested that he call a supervisor. He left and returned in about an hour and he said he misunderstood. He said there was a room air filter for the heating and air-conditioning system, but it was located in the hall. I said I didn't care where it was located, but I wanted a clean one installed. The next day he told me he changed it, and that was the last cold I had in that cabin.

My next and third illness came when I was transferred to a different cabin for the final leg of the voyage.

I had befriended a couple from Australia on a previous cruise. Lord Edward and Lady Margaret Pennington spoke to me with great emotion about the sickness and infection on the ship. Their reaction to avoid contamination was to cancel all shore excursions and remain in their room for the remainder of their cruise. They didn't even leave their room to eat at the restaurants. They used room service to order three meals a day. They washed the same utensils and glassware to avoid contamination from the ship's facilities. They asked the steward to not touch their tissues. The steward responded that he had to, as it was the ship's standard. The steward never touched the tissues again because for the remainder of their cruise he was denied entry to their room.

Due to the ever-present coughs, colds, and infections, the ship was nicknamed the *Floating Petri Dish.*

Chapter 2

SLAMMING BALCONY DOORS

Anyone who has enjoyed cruising on any other ship is immediately aware of the design flaws on this one. To get from fore to aft on well-designed ships, one would take the elevator to one of the main decks, which is usually on deck two or three. They would walk to the opposite end of the ship in a beautiful open area, usually abounding with pleasantly appointed shops, designs, and artwork. They then would take the elevator back to the deck sought. Aboard the *Dark Ship*, there is no convenient fore-to-aft "avenue." One must tramp through narrow tunnels of the enclosed cabin areas, meeting with musty cabin air and the aromas of toilet usage that permeate the passageways.

Also, when outside on an upper deck and wanting to walk down to a lower deck where the outdoor pools are, on this ship, one must go indoors and walk through areas with other activities. An example is wanting to use the pool on deck eight:

one must walk, wearing a bathing suit, and pass through a posh restaurant to gain access to the pool.

If a passenger is outdoors and desires to walk from an upper deck down to an outdoor pool using the outdoor route, he is stopped by a sign indicating not to descend the stairs because it is a reserved area for the higher paying guests. He then has to travel through the inner enclosed, small hallway route with all its stuffy discomfort.

In addition to the bothersome design flaws in the ship was the shoddy construction. On a previous world cruise I took on the *Queen Victoria*, the ship was so well constructed that I never heard noise from connecting cabins. On the world cruise aboard *Dark Ship*, the walls were paper thin. I could hear the TV from the adjoining room. On one cruise segment, my neighbor coughed horribly when he woke up in the morning, always around 9 a.m. On one occasion, I thought he was about to die. I could also hear a female voice, probably his wife, consoling him as he hacked and emitted his deathly sounds. It sounded like the poor man was near death.

When my balcony door closed, it would slam, sending vibrations to the connecting cabins. The noise was so disturbing that my neighbor knocked on my door and asked me not to slam my door. Because I love photography and made many trips out to my balcony to photograph birds and sunrises or sunsets, my slamming door became an annoyance. From the time of the complaint, I made a conscious effort to use my hand to impede the door slam. One night, when a sunset view made for an appealing photograph, I rushed inside for my camera, using my hand as a brake. Somehow, with my hand behind my back, I miscalculated the timing and my finger was caught in the slam. There was significant profanity to be heard. I assume it was heard as far away as the tenth-deck pool. There was bleeding, swelling, discoloration, and pain that wracked my finger.

This painful event brought me in contact with the medical procedures of *Dark Ship*. After washing my wound and using tissues to wrap my finger to stem the blood flow, I proceeded to the ship's infirmary. Upon arrival, I found myself in a short line behind an elderly German couple. In halting English, the man indicated to the woman at the desk that his wife was suffering chest pains, had difficulty breathing, and felt a numbness in her arm. I immediately recognized these as signs of a heart attack. I was shocked when the young woman behind the desk calmly handed the man a clipboard with numerous papers attached and told him to fill them out. She then turned her attention to me and asked what I wanted. I told her, "A Band-Aid." I explained, "I caught my finger in my balcony door, which seems to be in need of repair." I explained that my neighbor complained of the noise and as I tried to quiet the annoyance, I caught my finger. I held up my hand, with the bloody tissues as evidence, for her to see. Uninterested in the explanation, she reached across the desk and, with a bored look on her face, handed me a Band-Aid. I stood there, took the Band-Aid, looked at my other hand with bloody tissues, and told her that one would not be enough. She then reached across the desk and handed me another. I held the two Band-Aids and said, "This injury will be with me for a few days.

Could I have five?" With a bored look, she complied. As I was leaving, I sympathetically passed the German couple suffering a life-threatening event and observed them struggling with answering the questions written in English. I considered myself lucky. I got five Band-Aids and didn't have to fill out a clipboard full of forms and declarations. Throughout the remainder of the cruise I often wondered with sympathy what became of the unfortunate German couple.

As I returned to my cabin, I thought of how differently someone with the German woman's symptoms would be handled at a medical facility in the United States. The reaction would be immediate! The woman behind the desk would press a button. Alarms would sound, bells would ring, and claxons would wail. The response would be immediate! Medical staff from several directions would arrive at a run. They would be pushing a gurney, with an oxygen tank and numerous other life-saving devices. The woman's condition would be treated with the utmost seriousness.

But this was not a medical facility in the United States or any other competent medical facility around the world. This was the infirmary aboard the uncaring *Dark Ship.*

Because the source of my injured finger was not fixed, I was merely given five Band-Aids. I contacted the purser. I reported my slamming balcony door, my complaining German neighbor, and my injured finger with only five Band-Aids to help it heal. She listened intently and she too, like the woman behind the desk in the infirmary, ignored the comments about the complaining German neighbor and negligent infirmary and told me she would send a carpenter to check on the door.

I had three Band-Aids left when he arrived the next night and inspected the errant door. He opened it wide and let it go, permitting it to slam. He continued that routine for about five minutes, each time making minor adjustments to the mechanism. All this time I gritted my teeth, hoping my German neighbor was not in his room to hear the noise. My fear was soon realized, and my angry neighbor loudly knocked on my door. This time he was dressed in a bathrobe, which indicated to me that the noise woke him. He was far angrier than he was on his previous visit. I showed him my injured finger, explaining I got it trying to prevent the door's slamming because I didn't want to annoy him. He may not have understood English because he responded with some loud and angry words in German which I didn't understand. I reacted by opening my door wide to show him the mechanic working on the door. When he saw the man on a ladder tending to the door, he seemed disappointed. I believe he would have rather cursed me out in German than get a reasonable explanation for the noises.

After a dozen or so more slams, the mechanic indicated he had to order a new siphon—the device mounted above the door that slows its closing, thereby preventing the annoying slams, injured fingers, and angry, complaining neighbors.

Now I began to wonder how long it would take to order a mechanism that slows balcony doors from slamming. We were in the Indian Ocean between Goa and Sri Lanka. I thought of

Amazon back home with its convenient overnight deliveries. I wondered how long it would take before I could utilize my balcony without angering my neighbor or catching my finger again. I really didn't want to go back down to the infirmary and ask for more Band-Aids. I was pleasantly surprised when the mechanic returned the next night with a brand-new piston mechanism, designed to give me a quiet door, save the infirmary from giving out their precious Band-Aids, and appease my German neighbor.

It was such a delight! For two full days I was able to use my balcony without having my hand placed in peril. However, the tranquility derived from quiet door closings was short-lived. On the third day, the smooth-functioning door's performance ended. There came a noticeable, but not unreasonable noise. Two days later, the noise became louder, and by the fifth day the slamming was the same as before. I reported it and another mechanic arrived. He indicated the piston wasn't the problem at all. It was an old ship, he said, and that was the way the ship was designed. By design, many of the doors throughout the ship didn't fit properly. Ugh! Professional confirmation that *Dark Ship* was cursed from the start.

One of our waiters indicated the ship was built in modules. The modules were constructed in a factory, transported to the ship, and assembled at the shipyard. On paper, I'm sure the modules were precisely measured to a fraction of a millimeter on a blueprint and designed to fit perfectly. But somewhere, something became distorted. It reminded me of the Johnny Cash song, *One Piece at a Time.*

ALEXANDER FLINT

One Piece at a Time, by Wayne Kemp

Well, I left Kentucky back in forty-nine

An' went to Detroit workin' on a 'sembly line

The first year they had me putting wheels on Cadillacs

Every day I'd watch them beauties roll by

And sometimes I'd hang my head and cry

'Cause I always wanted me one that was long and black

One day I devised myself a plan

That should be the envy of most any man

I'd sneak it out of there with a lunchbox in my hand

Now getting caught meant getting fired

But I'd have it all by the time I retired

I'd have me a car worth at least a hundred grand

I'd get it one piece at a time

And it wouldn't cost me a dime

You'll know it's me when I come through your town

I'm gonna ride around in style

I'm gonna drive everybody wild

'Cause I'll have the only one there is around.

So the very next day when I punched in

With my big lunchbox and with help from my friends

I left that day with a lunchbox full of gears

I've never considered myself a thief

But GM wouldn't miss just one piece

Especially if I strung it out over several years.

The first day I got me a fuel pump

And the next day I got me an engine and a trunk

Then I got me a transmission and all the chrome

The little things I could get in my big lunchbox

Like nuts and bolts, and all four shocks

But the big stuff we snuck out in my buddy's mobile home

Well, up to now my plan went all right

Till we tried to put it together one night

And that's when we noticed that something was wrong.

The transmission was a fifty-three

And the motor turned out to be a seventy-three

And when we tried to put it together, all the holes were gone

So we drilled it out so that it would fit

And with a little help from an adapter kit

We had that engine runnin just like a song

Now the headlights were another sight

We had two on the left and one on the right

But when we pulled out the switch, all three of them come on

The back end looked kinda funny too

But we put it all together and when we got through

Well, that's when we noticed that we only had one tail fin.

About that time my wife walked out

And I could see in her eyes that she had her doubts

But she opened the door and said, "Honey, take me for a spin"

So we drove up town just to get the tags

And I headed her right on down the main drag

I could hear everybody laughin for blocks around

But up there at the court house they didn't laugh

'Cause to type it up took the whole staff

And when they got through, the title weighed sixty pounds

I got it one piece at a time

And it wouldn't cost me a dime

That song was about a man who worked in a Detroit Cadillac factory. At the beginning of his career, he began by bringing home one piece of the car home each night. He was planning that after a thirty-year career he would have enough parts to construct a car for himself. But when the man tried to put the car together, all the holes were gone. The hapless automotive worker didn't realize that every few years, the models changed their design.

I wonder what the excuse for poor fittings of the *Dark Ship's* modules *its* designers have to offer. The ill-fitting modules are annoyingly obvious on the ship. When walking through the passageways one will feel the uneven floor, indicating where one component didn't meet the other as precisely as it did on the drawing board.

Another miscalculation, I was told by the same waiter, was that the smokestacks were too tall and couldn't fit under some of the bridges where it had to sail. To the embarrassment of the designers, the stacks had to be cut to a lower height before the ship could sail into all ports. One explanation was that the ship's designers measured the distance between the water level and the bottom of the bridge at low tide. They never realized the water levels change every six hours with the tides.

Duh! Maybe the architects never built ships but only buildings on land that didn't have tides and bridges to consider.

The ship's design, however, was not the major complaint. The royal disgrace of the ship was in the management. Too many incidents of incompetence and human neglect were evident.

Although I was taking the entire world cruise, from New York to Peking and back to New York, my travel agent booked me for three separate segments. The ship sailed from New York to England, then England back to England, then England back to New York—three separate segments. I had three separate cabins. As a premium cruiser, I had taken many previous cruises with this cruise line, and I was supposed to get a gratis bottle of champagne for each segment. I only received a bottle on the first leg of my cruise.

Each of the three cabins came with its own problems. The first one was situated over the theater. At night when there was a show with music, my room vibrated from the bass speakers. It was quite annoying. The late show, which came after I had fallen asleep, was quite bothersome. I called the purser, who seemed to be expecting my call, and she was very understanding. She informed me she would ask the musical director to lower the volume on the bass speakers. She was ready for my complaint, had a sympathetic answer, and soothed me over. I later found out that had I demanded a new cabin, I would have been given one. There was no throbbing sound on following nights because that musical show was only given on the first night of the ocean-crossing segment.

On the middle segment of the cruise, which was ninety-five days long, I had problems with the slamming balcony door and noise from the adjoining cabins. This was explained in the previous chapter.

On the last segment of my world cruise, I was given a third cabin. This was an inside room without a balcony. I was unhappy with it, but it was one my travel agent booked to keep my costs down. This was the cabin where I was stricken with my third upper respiratory infection. It also presented design flaws my previous two cabins didn't have. It was a smaller cabin, which allowed me less room to maneuver in. Since it was designed with a smaller square footage, there was less room for storage. The largest items I had to store were my luggage. My two previous cabins had been wisely planned; the space under the bed was to be used as storage space. That was where my luggage neatly fit. In the inside cabin, with smaller square footage, the planners somehow had arranged for the bed to be designed so close to the floor that no luggage could fit under it. Underbed storage space was lacking where storage space was needed most. Duh! Didn't any one of the ship's administrators think of a simple way to raise the bed a few inches? The carpenter's shop could easily fashion blocks of wood to be placed under the legs of the bed so it could be utilized as a storage space for luggage. Again, the incompetency and lack of thought by the management astound me.

While in this third, and last of cabins, the management, thinking I just boarded in England, recognized me as a newly embarked passenger. The mandatory announcement for a lifeboat drill was announced the first day of the Atlantic crossing. I had been on the same ship for several months. I called the purser and asked if I had to attend. I was told if I did the drill on the last segment, which I did, I was not required to attend. I remained in my room during the announcements to report to a certain location and did not appear for the lifeboat drill. A few minutes prior to the drill, my cabin steward entered my cabin and told me I had to attend the drill. I explained I had been on board for several months and I had just checked with the purser and she said I didn't have to attend.

When I returned from dinner that night, I found a letter of reprimand in my mail slot. It indicated I missed the mandatory safety session and had to attend a makeup class. That was the first of a long line of warnings, threats, and directives that I had to attend the punishment class. Every time I called and explained my situation, the person on the other end of the call told me all was okay. Whenever that happened, I was sent another stern letter indicating all newly arrived passengers had to attend the lifeboat drill. This is more evidence that the lines of communication on this ship were poor. When I went to the punishment class, I told the officer in charge of the class of my plight. He understood and indicated for me to put my name on the attendance list and I could leave.

What I found amazing was that the ship's administrators recognized me as a new passenger in need of the safety instruction. The same administration, however, didn't recognize me as a new passenger when it came time to award me a bottle of champagne. I was a preferred passenger due to my dozen previous cruises with the same cruise line. Shame on them for not recognizing me as such.

Chapter 3

THE ART TEACHER FROM HELL

Ever since my first voyage in 2012, which was a beautiful cruise of the Baltic Sea, I have enjoyed the watercolor painting classes. It was on the *Queen Elizabeth* that I met the wonderful art teacher Gina Strumpf, a professional artist from Charleston, South Carolina. I had never painted before I took Gina's class. She taught, encouraged, and guided me to become an artist. I am forever grateful to her. I had about ten other teachers on different cruises, and all were good. One other excellent teacher stands out in my memory. Mary Gordon was knowledgeable and had a wonderful teaching personality. I consider Gina and Mary to be among my lifetime friends.

This world cruise, which began in January and ended in April, I will remember as the voyage from hell. It is only fitting that the art teacher, her personality, and her abilities would be commensurate with the horrors of that cruise.

A middle-aged woman, she was quite short, with her width equal to her height. When she spoke to the class, she spoke ever so slowly, so slowly that I thought I was back in kindergarten. It was just the way Miss Day spoke to me on my first day of school in PS 160 in Brooklyn, New York. In addition, Mrs. Short Round possessed a disciplinary nature. She insisted that the participants in her class mark all their art supplies with their names. When she wasn't speaking in her nauseatingly slow manner, she would patrol the class looking for a paintbrush or ruler without a name on it. When she found one, she would hold it up and shame the miscreant. The owner, a paying passenger, didn't deserve to be humiliated or treated so poorly. She gave me the idea that she was trying to drive down the numbers of her students by encouraging them to drop out. In that effort, she was successful.

In her opening speech, she laid down the strict rules for her class. I never experienced any controlling threats in the dozen or so art classes I enjoyed on previous cruises. She said if any of the students needed an item of art equipment, like a ruler, they had to sign for it. Just like a book from a library. There was a blue sign-out sheet for certain art teaching lessons, and pink sheets for other painting instructions. If an art class participant wanted to read her painting tips, they were required to sign for them. At the end of this speech, the class was reminded, in a loud and threatening manner, "These are not for you to keep, they belong to me and not to you, so you will return them at the end of each class. Anyone who does not return an item will be hunted down and made to return it." She actually said "hunted down."

I wonder why she didn't use the ship's copy machine to print the art lesson and give it to the students to keep. That way she would be like all the other competent teachers I enjoyed on my other cruises. Perhaps, I think, she enjoyed flaunting her corpulent authority.

In addition to her annoying demeanor, and this is unforgivable, she would do her best to rid her class of students. Any teacher knows it's simpler and more pleasant to have a small class than a large one.

On the fourth day of the class, I heard a new student request to join. The teacher indicated that she was too late, the class was all filled up. The woman responded that there were only five students present and many empty seats. Ms. Teacher, in her slow-talking manner, showed the prospective student the sign-in clipboard. The class roster indicated that there were thirty students signed up. In a slow, deliberate speech, Mrs. Slow Talker demonstrated her benevolence by saying she was only required to accept twenty-five students, but out of kindness, she personally allowed thirty to register. She did not reveal that she, with her obnoxious personality, drove off the large number of students, thus leaving her with a smaller and simpler class to manage. Never before in any cruise ship art class did I see an art teacher turn a prospective student down. They always found room.

Her obnoxious behavior drove me away too. I had enough of her and dropped out, seeking other delights that my $38,000 world cruise would offer. My hope was that when that first segment of the cruise ended, a new art teacher would come aboard. However, on the first day of each new cruise segment, when I eagerly checked in the Daily Program, I was hugely disappointed to see that Ms. Arrogant Slow Talker remained aboard for each new segment. Sadly, she was present for the entire ninety-five days of the world cruise, England to England. I was free of her only on the two seven-day Atlantic crossings.

Among the best memories of my twelve previous cruises that I enjoyed prior to *Dark Ship* were from the various watercolor art classes. As I mentioned at the beginning of this chapter, I credit my first experience with watercolors to Gina. That was on a Baltic Sea cruise aboard the *Queen Elizabeth*. Gina Stumpf showed great patience and talent as a teacher. Her professional art is world class.

On another cruise aboard the *Queen Victoria*, I was pleased to take the class of another wonderful art teacher. Mary Gordon was able to bring out hidden talents in her students.

Having an art teacher that not only is below quality, but one who displays such unprofessional behavior was greatly disappointing for me. I was told that several students complained to the purser about the obnoxious actions of *Dark Ship's* art teacher. It seems the complaints were ignored because she remained aboard for three months, the entire world cruise, England to England. Ugh!

Chapter 4

ESCAPE FROM THE CASSEROLE QUEENS

"I'm an Ordinary Man" from *My Fair Lady* by songwriters Alan Jay Lerner and Frederick Loewe

I'm an ordinary man

Who desires nothing more than just an

ordinary chance

To live exactly as he likes and do precisely what he

wants

An average man am I, of no eccentric whim

Who likes to live his life free of strife

Doing whatever he thinks is best for him

Well, just an ordinary man

But, let a woman in your life

And your serenity is through

She'll redecorate your home, from cellar to the

dome

And then go on to the enthralling fun of overhauling

You

Let a woman in your life

And you're up against the wall

Make a plan and you will find she has

Something else in mind

And spend it searching for her glove

Let a woman in your life

I'm an ordinary man

Who desires nothing more than just an ordinary

Chance

To live exactly as he likes and do precisely what he wants

An average man am I, of no eccentric whim

Who likes to live his life free of strife

Doing whatever he thinks is best for him

Well, just an ordinary man.

But, let a woman in your life

And your serenity is through

She'll redecorate your home from cellar to the dome

And then go on to the enthralling fun of overhauling you

Let a woman in your life and you're up against a wall

Make a plan and you will find she has

something else in mind

And so rather than do either, you do something else

That neither likes at all

You want to talk of Keats and Milton

She wants to talk of love

You go to see a play or ballet

And spend it searching for her glove

Let a woman in your life

And you invite eternal strife

Let them buy their wedding bands

For those anxious little hands

I'd be equally as willing

For a dentist to be drilling

Than to ever let a woman in my life

I'm a very gentle man

Even-tempered and good-natured who you never hear complain

Who has the milk of human kindness by the quart in every vein

A patient man am I, down to my fingertips

The sort who never would, never could

Let an insulting remark escape his lips

A very gentle man

But let a woman in his life

And patience hasn't got a chance

She will beg you for advice, your reply will

be concise and she'll listen very nicely, and then go out and do

Precisely what she wants

You are a man of grace and polish

Who never spoke above a hush

Now all at once you're using language

That would make a sailor blush

Let a woman in your life

And your sabbatical is through

In a line that never ends comes an army of her friends

Come to jabber and to chatter

And tell her what the matter is with you

She'll have a booming boisterous family

Who will descend on you en masse

She'll have a large Wagnerian mother

With a voice that shatters glass

Let a woman in your life?

Let a woman in your life?

I shall never let a woman in my life

A single straight man who is happy with his status has the dreaded task of politely deflecting the onslaught of ravenous divorcees and widows, many of whom are actively engaged in methods of altering his happy position. Yes, these women conspire to adhere to a man with their hungry, selfish tentacles. I know, because I have had to use my vast skills and street-smart abilities to remain happily single. This battle constantly wages in the vast canyon of high-rise condos and the network of gated adult communities throughout the world. It is nonstop. They have been referred to as the *Baker's Brigade, the Casserole Queens, She Wolves,* and the *Lady Spiders.* These women are relentless. The *Dark Ship's* passenger base was no different.

Aboard the *Dark Ship*, a man from Alabama told me how he was deceived into taking this cruise. He was told by a widowed neighbor that a group from his gated community, the large group of seniors he socialized with, were going on a cruise together. As a person who enjoyed cruising on luxury cruise ships, and happy to spend time in the company of his friends, he went home and immediately booked passage.

It wasn't until a week before the cruise that he learned the scheming spider had entrapped him in her web. It was just the two of them from their community taking this cruise. When he confronted her as to the deviance in plans, she indicated that she merely assumed they were all attending. When he asked the other members of the group, he found out they never knew anything about it. He was ensnared. He departed on the cruise thinking he would spend the time at sea enjoying his own pursuits. He was wrong! He discovered she was quite adept at finding him wherever he sought refuge. He secretly booked several excursions for when the ship was in port. He didn't know how, but she always found him. An intelligent man, he vowed never to have that situation ensnare him again.

Another story, told by a friend from the gym, was about being invited to a dinner party in his adult gated community. He was also led to believe a group of friends would be present. He dutifully purchased orange juice to mix with a bottle of champagne to make mimosas. In addition he brought along a bouquet of flowers for the group to enjoy. He anticipated a pleasant gathering among his friends. Upon entering her apartment, he was glad that he purchased the expensive champagne because he immediately recognized the vast preparations the hostess made. There were candles lit, incense burning, and the smells of delightful food emanating from the oven. He was disappointed to discover the dinner party would only include himself and the lady who prepared it. Aha, the devious spider, the casserole queen and a member of the baker's brigade all wrapped in one hungry female. My friend experienced his first devious web of entrapment.

While aboard *Dark Ship*, and after spending the evening on the dance floor with an attractive widow from the Bronx, I was offered a proposal. She told me she liked me, would like me to live with her, and would be my "nurse with a purse." I had never heard that term before and asked her to explain it. She clarified that I fit the image of what she would desire. Because she was younger than I, she assumed I would fall into ill health before she would, and so could be my nurse. Also, she pointed out in the same breath, she was financially stable, owned two homes, one in Florida, and would like to include me in her life, offering financial support. After digesting what she had just proposed, I gave her credit for her honesty. I told her I was flattered but was not in need of a financial purse. I explained that due to the healthy genes inherited from my parents, I didn't expect the need for a nurse for a long time. In addition, I was content with my single status.

While on a golf excursion on the cruise, one of my foursome told the story of receiving a call from a neighbor in his Arizona condo, asking if she could come down to spend the night with him. When he hesitated, she said she was frightened by a severe thunderstorm and would appreciate his company for a while. He told her she could stop by, assuming it would be until the storm passed. The knock on the door revealed other plans were in store for him. He was greeted by a widow in a revealing nightgown who immediately threw her arms around him and snuggled closely. His hormones began to flow, and the outcome was as would be expected. They certainly slept together that night. Although he was pleased at having a neighbor with benefits, he soon realized she was deluded into believing they were a couple.

Another male friend on the ship told a story of a woman in his Savannah, Georgia, retirement community. She warned all the other single women in the community to stay away from him. She had her sights set on him and didn't want any competition. We then wondered if there was a vast network, maybe a web of widows that conspired to ensnare a happy single male.

Several men in the group soon realized why they were more comfortable with lesbian friends.

Chapter 5

A Plea For Blood

I n the second week of April, as the ship was nearing Lisbon, the captain made a ship-wide announcement. That is, the announcement came through *all* the ship's speakers. Usually announcements are blasted only in common areas and not in cabins. The ship's cabins are never disturbed except to fulfill international laws like the ship's mandatory lifeboat drill at the beginning of the journey. They would also be used in an emergency, when it may be deemed necessary to enter lifeboats to abandon ship. So, all passengers recognized the announcement as something serious.

That evening, in a solemn voice, the captain announced there was an emergency on the ship. He said that type 0 positive blood was urgently needed. Any passengers with that blood type were requested to immediately report to the infirmary.

It was the first time I ever heard of the ship's captain asking the passengers for their blood. In the absence of an explanation, rumors quickly circulated regarding the need for such an announcement. We were in friendly waters, and well away from the countries where pirates are a threat. All we could assume was that there was a horrible accident or an illness for which the blood was needed.

I eagerly awaited an announcement the next morning to hear a follow-up regarding the unusual request. We all expected it to come in the morning. It did not. At the noon report the following day, I stopped what I was doing, as did many other passengers, and listened intently to the captain's account of the ship's status. Nothing of the blood request was mentioned. We didn't expect a comprehensive description, because illnesses and deaths are never explained in detail, but we listened intently expecting some sort of an account.

We did not expect the incident to be ignored by the captain in his noon report. We expected a "thank you for the magnificent turnout to donate," or reassuring apology for the strange request.

When something of great interest is ignored, it allows for wild rumors to abound. Well, *Dark Ship's* dark behavior was no different. Someone said there were both kitchen personnel and passengers as victims due to a violent knife attack by a cook. Another rumor held that a newly embarked African worker suffered from hemorrhagic fever, which caused him to endure a severe loss of blood. Others said it was a work-related accident involving a beef mincing machine that severed an arm. That rumor prompted a table mate to swear off hamburgers for the rest of the cruise. Another rumor spread that it was an exotic disease, possibly dengue fever, bubonic plague, or Ebola. Still another had to do with a passenger suffering from bleeding intestines due to swallowing broken glass from food in the buffet, placed there by a disgruntled kitchen worker.

Ignoring this issue was pure ignorance and negligence on the part of the captain. It was too big an incident to ignore.

Similarly, the captain again dropped the ball when he neglected to enlighten the passengers after another of his panicked announcements. It occurred when we were about to leave Tianjin, China. It was six in the evening and we were gathered around our dining table in the restaurant. Annmarie noted that we hadn't sailed yet. We were scheduled to sail at 5 p.m. It was about an hour late and we felt that the tour bus to Peking was probably late arriving from its twelve-hour journey. About an hour later, as we were eating our main course, we heard another announcement. It was a request for a group of guests, about eight passengers, to call the purser. This usually occurred when guests who left the ship were not accounted for. In the past, it was usually a short time later and the sounds of the ship untying from the dock were heard. The perception of being under way followed shortly thereafter. On this occasion, there was no feeling of the ship untying, but the names were called again. A few minutes later the captain, in a frantic voice, read the names and indicated they should immediately report to the purser. This was unusual. We had never heard the captain's voice calling for people who were somehow misplaced. Often, they were found never to have left the ship in the first place. He called names two more times and each time the list was smaller. After about an hour, the captain again came on the loudspeaker to announce the Chinese authorities found irregularities on the passports of the eight passengers and had to visibly see them before the ship would be allowed to leave the port.

The captain sounded annoyed at the Chinese for waiting until the last minute to issue their order. He indicated that the delay was so long, we had lost our place in the shipping lane. In waiting for a new spot to get in the sailing lane, we would be late to our destination the following day. Therefore, he said, some of the morning excursions in Kitakyushu, Japan, would have to be cancelled.

It was our belief that *Dark Ship's* personnel were somehow again negligent in their duties. The captain used the Chinese to shift blame from his own negligence in being late for the next day's activities.

Chapter 6

FIXING THE PROBLEMS

At table 357 during the early seating, six world cruise passengers, who had been together for nearly two months, discussed the cruise line's and ship's shortcomings. How could these issues be resolved?

Firstly, they concluded the initial boarding procedure was where the complaints began. Bringing back unpleasant memories, they recalled entering a huge warehouse-like area. A declaration had to be signed before entering the cruise terminal asserting you had no infectious diseases and were devoid of all contaminating illnesses. Now the fallacy here is that after waiting sometimes up to a year or more after booking the cruise and arranging his schedule, a person is not going to jeopardize his dream by declaring that he has a cold or is suffering from diarrhea. He is going to sign the brief declaration indicating he is well and enter the hall.

At this point in the cruise terminal, there is a long, controlled line with numerous convoluted turns. Like in an airport, the passenger crawls along as the line moves slowly forward until the front of the line is reached. He is now greeted by a long, chest-high desk, behind which are seated numerous agents from the cruise line. The check-in procedure now begins. He is asked for his boarding pass, which was printed out on his computer prior to leaving his house. His passport is then collected and retained by the cruise line. His photograph is taken. Several other forms are signed, and he is made to wait for his room's keycard to be manufactured. This room key also acts as his charge card. His credit card is scrutinized, recorded, and checked for its validity. This takes many minutes after he has already waited in the long, snaking line before approaching this desk. Finally, he is given his room key and sent on his way. Thinking he is about to board the ship, he is soon disappointed because he enters another large waiting zone. If lucky, he may get a seat where he must continue to wait. The new boarding passenger is now in the company of hundreds of other irritable, impatient, waiting passengers. This wait, where one may be forced to stand if all the seats are taken, is a horror. Sometimes this delay can be an hour or more until the cabins are declared ready. Remember now, the passenger has already gone through a stressful ordeal negotiating the previous lines. In addition, many passengers are at the end of a long journey, many flying thousands of miles to arrive at the cruise terminal. They have spent many hours, perhaps days, since they packed their luggage and departed their homes. Throughout this monstrous ordeal, while in the cruise terminal, there are numerous agents of the cruise line directing people where to go, where to sit, and cajoling the passengers into thinking they will board shortly. Never does anyone indicate how long "shortly" is.

Last year I took a cruise on Royal Caribbean's *Symphony of the Seas.* I wanted to experience the largest and newest cruise ship afloat. With six thousand passengers, more than twice the number of passengers on any ship I had previously sailed, I expected a horror show. But, to my pleasant surprise, their procedures were distinctly different. I was astonished because the many redundant, annoying habits of the cruise line I had previously sailed were absent. The aggravation, impatience, and long lines of the cruise terminal were nonexistent. There was no snaking line, no long desk manned by cruise line agents. There was no secondary waiting area, no room key waiting time. No numerous cruise line agents, on the payroll, abounding everywhere. There was no cruise terminal registration!

Royal Caribbean has a system where, in the comfort of my home, I registered using my own computer. It was from home that I registered my credit card, gave my passport information, and enacted all necessary boarding procedures. I then printed out my boarding pass, which contained a bar code. As I stepped on the ship, the security agent scanned my bar code and took a photo of me and welcomed me aboard. I asked for my room pass and was told it was in the room. Nothing was between me and my room but three decks and an elevator. It took me ten minutes to get from the curbside in Miami to my room, where a chilled bottle of champagne was awaiting me.

Simplicity—what a concept! I wonder if *Dark Ship's* cruise line ever considered any of Royal Caribbean's strategies? Think of all the shoreside personnel in the cruise terminal who would not have to be hired. Also, there was no waiting in long lines, and no fatigued, irritable passengers. Why, I wonder, why doesn't the antiquated cruise line adapt?

Another huge change that Royal Caribbean employs is in dealing with shore excursions. Aboard *Dark Ship*, I experienced the lack of efficiency when I booked a shore excursion. The excursion passenger, at the time indicated on his ticket, must report to a large waiting area. It may be in a restaurant or a bar, but the theater is primarily used. However, to get to the waiting area, one must negotiate huge lines or queues, as the British refer to them. Very often the lines snake around the hallways before they get to the entrance of the theater meeting place. Sometimes people arrive at the entrance to the theater via a staircase that does not always bring them to the end of the line. There is no ship's company to direct traffic. When the individuals descending the stairs enter the line, it is not at the end but in the middle somewhere. The people waiting in line from the end of it will often show their annoyance at what they perceive as line jumpers, and they are quick to offer rude comments. The line enters the theater, where colored stickers are given out to match people with their tour. When the tour number is called, passengers are led by a ship's personnel who, for visibility, holds a tall pole with the tour number affixed to it. He then leads his followers to the tour bus in a parking lot, somewhere off the ship. Sometimes the leader with the pole number outdistances those following him due to crowds and queues waiting to enter the theater. It is at this point that many trailing passengers become lost. This always adds to the confusion and delays the tour. When luck abounds, those in the following line will arrive at the tour bus in due time.

Just a note, aboard *Dark Ship*, there were never any ship's personnel around to guide the masses in properly negotiating the queues as they approached the theater. Remember, passengers await their colored stickers in the theater waiting area. If there were ship's staff present, there would not be the anger and drama from those waiting in line when they are trying to enter the theater.

None of this commotion occurred on the Royal Caribbean's 6,000-passenger *Symphony of the Seas*. The number of passengers was more than double that of those aboard *Dark Ship*. Their solution was so simple, I wouldn't believe it had I not witnessed it. They don't stage and organize the excursion tours in any theater, restaurant, or ballroom on board the ship. Similar to *Dark Ship*, Royal Caribbean distributes the tour tickets to the room. After hearing their tour number called, the passengers then depart the ship. The tickets have a number indicating where to meet the organizers of the tour they signed up for. This is off the ship! It is on the dock! Simplicity, what a concept!

No more confusion and energy wasted while looking for the meeting place on the ship, like a restaurant or a theater. No more colored stickers. No more long lines of passengers coming from different directions and conflicting with one another to find the theater. The challenge of following a ship's personnel holding a pole with the tour number is nonexistent. Again, had I not seen this procedure, I would not have believed it. It worked! The tour number was called, and the passengers left their cabins, disembarked the ship, arrived on the dock, and then walked down the dock until they saw their tour number, plainly displayed by the tour leader. They then signed their name on a clipboard. When all the members registered for the tour were present, the passengers followed the tour leader to the bus and proceeded on their way. Duh! It was so simple. I was shocked at how, for the twelve cruises I took with *Dark Ship's* cruise line, I had followed the complicated procedure I thought was unavoidable. Simplicity, what a concept!

To enable the queue or line to debark efficiently, Royal Caribbean had a crew member strategically located prior to the debarkation desk where the room card would be scanned. The crew member would ask to see the room card to ensure the passenger had his room card in his hand ready for scanning to debark. After debarkation, he would be directed to his tour gathering place. On *Dark Ship* that crew member was not present. The passengers often did not have their room cards out and in hand, but had to search for it, thereby stalling the debarkation procedure. On *Dark Ship*, I witnessed a debarking passenger being asked for his identification card who did not have it in his hand. He then had to hold up the debarkation procedure to remove his backpack. He had to open the backpack to remove his wife's purse. After fumbling through her purse, the wife found her card and had it scanned. Then she left the ship. The husband, who put his backpack back on, then realized he did not remove his own card. So, the backpack again had to be removed, again holding up the departing line. The backpack had to be fumbled through once more until his card was found. Mr. Clueless never realized he was holding up numerous passengers eager to debark. We realized this because he took his time putting his backpack back on, adjusted it for comfort, and then casually proceeded to leave the ship. All this time, the flow of exiting passengers was stopped and everyone in the line had to wait for his delay. Had *Dark Ship's* cruise line stationed a crew member in a strategic location near the end of the line, and asked to see the necessary card prior to reaching the exit station, the exiting delay could have been avoided. Multiply that delay by every few passengers and you can see why *Dark Ship's* debarkations were always so slow. Royal Caribbean had the crew member properly positioned, thus insuring a quicker debarkation. Duh again! Simplicity—what a concept!

What is wrong with *Dark Ship's* management? Was it their incompetent mismanagement or their lack of management? A rumor circulated among the passengers that the cruise line had enacted a money-saving procedure by eliminating many middle management positions. If true, the policy was a failure, as evidenced by the numerous sick and unhappy, disorganized and demoralized passengers. Enduring the mishaps aboard *Dark Ship*, many passengers swore they would never cruise with *Dark Ship's* cruise line again. Let's hope the failure is soon recognized and rectified.

Another bad experience I suffered was at the cruise sales office. In the first days of the world cruise, I desired to book a short cruise from New York to Canada. I arrived early but found there was a passenger ahead of me who was booking a future cruise. Seated just outside the office, I was able to overhear the entire process. After several minutes, I was able to hear the transaction come to its conclusion. By this time there were three other passengers seated next to me with the same intention of booking a cruise. I gathered the items I took to read while I waited and was ready to enter the office. I was wrong to believe that the ship's agent would be eager to get to his next customer. Unlike any other transaction where I was ready to spend a large amount of money to the benefit of the cruise line, I was wrong. It seemed that was when the agent decided to engage in a lengthy conversation with the passenger. It was a conversation that seemed like it went on forever. It included the weather, the hometown of the passenger, and the agent showing the knowledge he had of the area. He then launched into a story of someone he knew who lived in that area of England. About this time I stood up to let the agent know there was a line of passengers waiting to enter and spend their money, which would be to the benefit of the cruise line. The agent, who saw me waiting to enter his office, did not take the hint; he just continued his banal discussion with the previous customer. Standing in the doorway, I displayed my impatience, shifting from one foot to the other, looking at my watch and glancing at the ceiling to signal the agent to end his discussion. I wonder what the agent was thinking. After more than ten minutes of standing in view of the agent, I finally had enough. I turned and indicated to the other impatient customers still seated behind me, "That's it, I've had enough. I'll sail with another cruise line," and I left. Little did I know that this would be the precursor of a horrid cruise.

Chapter 7

Designing the Interior of a Cursed Ship

I n the first ten minutes aboard *Dark Ship*, I spewed forth a string of unmentionable words, which is unusual for me. I was in my cabin and unpacking, taking clothes from my luggage and neatly placing them in the drawers of the cabin. After filling the first drawer, I closed it with the intention of opening the drawer below it. Well, the silence was broken with a scream of pain. My finger was trapped in the drawer pull.

The design of the drawer pulls allow one's finger to fit behind it but not to be released. When an unsuspecting passenger closes the drawer and traps their finger, the result is significant pain. My own ensuing scream could be heard as far as the deck eight outdoor pool. Many times upon hearing mysterious screams about the ship, I attributed it to those pesky drawer pulls. This annoyance is avoidable by using common sense, and by attaching user-friendly drawer pulls to the cabin furniture.

Now somewhere in the vast educational systems of the globe, I am sure there is a course in designing dresser drawer handles. It seems logical that drawer handles should be made to function so efficiently that they don't cause injurious pain to the user. Additional thought must be given to a ship's furniture design because ships are often out to sea. Sometimes the seas are rough, and passengers sometimes lose their balance. Hopefully the passenger times his furniture use for when the seas are calm. Losing one's balance on a rolling sea with a finger wedged inside a poorly designed drawer pull could be a disaster worthy of a visit to an orthopedic surgeon. Again, I wonder, who made the design decisions aboard *Dark Ship*?

Apparently, the interior designers of *Dark Ship* did not take that course. If they had an understanding of human anatomy, they would have designed the pull differently. They would have followed the basic rule to not cause injurious pain to the user.

Another item the ship's designers missed was the installation of proper electrical outlets. What they needed were electrical outlets where all the plugs could be utilized. What they installed were outlets where the plugs were placed too close together. Every other outlet could not be used because the plugs to the devices utilizing them overlapped the outlet beside it. The negligence was astounding! Who was responsible for this stupendous error in planning? I wonder if any experts were hired, or if there was merely one architect. Is this evidence of a cost-cutting strategy? If so, I'm sure there are many passengers who swore they would never vacation with this cruise line again.

Another item of interior cabin design that is missing is a simple hanging hook on the wall. This helpful item has been available on all the other cruise ships I have frequented but is not to be found on *Dark Ship*. A hanging hook is useful when clothing is returned from the cleaners. When the cabin steward hangs it there, it serves notice by its visibility that your clothes have been returned. Also, a hook is helpful when preparing formal clothing for a function or for dinner. It would be a simple thing for the cruise line to install hooks, and that would go a long way to make the passengers' lives more pleasant. But then, this is the *Dark Ship*. It holds true to the thought that the passengers' comfort is the last thing the cruise line is thinking about.

Most passengers have devices that require charging batteries. This necessitates the availability of electrical outlets in the cabin. *Dark Ship* provides these necessary outlets, but they are placed so close together, the plugs take up the space of the outlets alongside them. With a computer, a cell phone, electric razor, a camera, and, for some travelers, a CPAP machine, passengers require user-friendly electrical outlets. A CPAP is a device to help a person with sleep apnea. They have to wear it when they sleep. Due to the poor design and placement of the electric outlets installed on the ship, the devices cannot be utilized effectively. When a sleep apnea patient boards the ship, he must remember to bring an extension cord because the electrical outlets are too far from the bed.

In addition, there are no electrical outlets in the bathroom. I can understand the fear of an electrical razor falling into a basin of water, the fear and risk of electrocution or fire. For the information of *Dark Ship's* management, there is a simple device for use in bathrooms and kitchens where water contacting electrical current can pose such a risk. They are called ground fault interrupters. I bought one recently at Home Depot for $7.00; not a huge expense. These safety devices immediately shut off the electrical flow when water touches the contacts.

While we are pondering the ship's design, perhaps at this point there should be a mention of the restaurant's design. The second and third deck make up the main dining facility located toward the rear of the ship. The kitchen is below the restaurant's two decks. After the orders are taken from the passengers, the waiter then goes down to the kitchen below and must wait in a line behind other waiters to gather the meals and bring them up to the table. In theory everything works well if everything works well. But as we know, Murphy's Law states, "If anything can go wrong, it will go wrong." Well, on *Dark Ship*, Murphy's Law abounds.

A passenger often changes his mind after the orders are delivered, refuses the food, and orders another dish. Or a passenger who decides to refuse a course sees a tablemate's order after it is delivered and decides to order the dish he initially refused. That means the assistant waiter must neglect his other duties and go back down two decks below. He then waits in a line, gathers up another meal, and returns two floors above to serve the oblivious passenger. Very often the passenger will ask, "What took you so long?" Frequently, the last thought a cruise passenger has on his mind is the plight of his waiter. He is thinking about his attire, what he is going to say, how he is going to impress his tablemates, and what he is going to order for dinner. His thoughts are not about the waiter's well-being.

I believe, with better planning by the ship's designers, there could have been a kitchen located closer to the restaurant. All my tablemates agreed that we never experienced restaurant delays on any other ship such as those evidenced aboard *Dark Ship*.

On previous cruises, one of my favorite activities was the theater. I love the various shows, the music and dancers. The stage productions were always a delight to experience. On *Dark Ship*, the theater was actually a painful chore to endure.

A few years after the ship was launched, the theater was redesigned. Someone sold the ship's administrators on the idea to install a new seating project. The color is tasteful, but the seating design is abominable. Most of the seats are without armrests. This is not comfortable for me. I have a painful back and need armrests to support my body weight. In addition, the material covering these seats without armrests is slippery. I continually slide down in the seat, making for great discomfort to my already painful back. Armrests would help from sliding. It seems the designers paid no attention to ergonomics. The human body needs a seat with a specific shape. *Dark Ship* has the most uncomfortable seats I have ever experienced, not only in this theater, but anywhere. Because of the actual pain

I felt in their seats, I attended the theater only twice. I would rather give up seeing a show than have discomfort and pain caused by *Dark Ship's* poorly designed theater seats.

It also seems the designers didn't consider passengers moving down the length of the ship. On all other ships, it was possible to travel from fore to aft and vice versa without having to walk along the cabin's hallways. It is far more pleasant to walk in public areas that have high ceilings with beautiful surroundings. This may include shops, restaurants, artwork, and statues.

On *Dark Ship*, to travel from one end of the ship to the other, the passengers are forced to walk long distances through the cramped cabin hallways. These are narrow tunnels with low ceilings that pass along the living quarters of the passengers. This is annoying when someone is walking in front of you at a slow pace. You are trapped behind them and forced to walk at their pace. Also, when foot traffic is walking toward you, you must create a narrow profile by walking as slow as possible and turning sideways to permit the person to pass you.

Very often these hallways are crammed with dirty sheets, cleaning gear, and appliances like vacuum cleaners. On other ships, there are alternatives available for traversing the ship, like an outdoor deck or an enjoyable way to travel along a common deck with high ceilings and pleasant shops.

On *Dark Ship*, to get to a pool and jacuzzi on the eighth deck, one must travel through an upscale restaurant. Imagine having to walk through a restaurant where passengers are wearing formal dress and you are merely wearing a bathing suit covered by a bathrobe, or as the British call it, "a dressing gown."

Not well thought out by the ship designers, indeed.

Chapter 8

INDIAN SECURITY

The ship arrived in Cochin, India, and no shuttle buses were provided. The only buses were for tours, where a seat must be booked in advance.

The Indian Taxi Mafia will not allow transportation to be provided by the ship. They feel it would cost them money and then they could not charge the ship's passengers their inflated taxi fares. This highlights the weakness of the cruise line's negotiation tactics when they arrange for the ship to visit a port. A cruise ship's visit to a country brings thousands of visitors for a day's visit. These vacationers are eager to spend money in that port—dining, visits to interesting sites, gifts for friends and family, and clothing for themselves. The money being spent is a boon to the country's economy. Most of the countries visited are significantly poor and benefit from money being spent there. One would think the country would be happy to host a cruise ship. If the cruise ship's executives were intelligent, an asset visibly lacking among *Dark Ship's* management, they could bargain with the country's bureaucrats who say the ship cannot have their free shuttle buses. These shuttle buses are hired from local companies, thus giving money to the locals. The economy of the country stands to benefit anyway. The taxi driver mafia in some countries like India overrules the country's officials and prevents the hiring of shuttle buses. This increases the burden on the ship's passengers. I hold the cruise line's administrators responsible for allowing their passengers to suffer the hardship of dealing with the bullying taxi mafia.

The cruise ship's managers who negotiate the berthing of the ship should realize that they, the cruise line managers, are in control. The ultimate power they have is to visit another port and deny the bullying country to be visited by their money spending passengers. *Dark Ship's* negotiators apparently never read the book *The Art of the Deal* by Donald Trump. The ship's executives appear to have been intimidated into accepting an agreement that is detrimental to their passengers. Shame on this cruise line's weak negotiators. It appears the *Dark Ship's* cruise line executives are lacking in the art of negotiation, among other things.

In the port of Cochin, India, I elected not to hire a cab at the Jesse James highway robbery rates and decided to walk to the local vendors located near the wharf. They were within sight of my balcony on the ship. There were dozens of stalls with colorful merchandise displayed and varying assortments of gifts. I spotted clothing, mostly women's dresses and scarfs. There also was a large selection of Indian jewelry at inexpensive prices. Other stalls sold tea and spices. In addition, there were many sought-after Indian items, like handmade quilts, saris, pashmina and cashmere shawls.

I visited several stalls, negotiated prices, and purchased everything I liked. I was always able to tell when I paid too much because I was given a gift of a tee shirt or extra shawl by the proprietor. I didn't mind overpaying because I felt these hardworking and friendly people could use the extra few rupees.

I felt satisfied when I headed back toward the ship along the unpaved, sandy roadway. The sky was a deep blue, the air was clear, and it was a comfortable temperature. I had a great feeling of accomplishment as I walked back to the ship. I was thinking of whom I would give the jewelry, and who would be gifted the scarfs and shawls. I have four daughters and one daughter-in-law. In addition, I'm blessed with five granddaughters. They all wear necklaces, bracelets, and earrings. Also, I made sure I purchased enough scarfs so everyone could get two or more. Yes, I was feeling quite satisfied.

I wore open-toed sandals along the sandy walkway and realized I would need a shower when I returned to my cabin. Little did I know that the thoughts of gift distribution and dusty feet would soon be the least of my soon-to-occur ship problems.

I boarded the ship and entered the security check-in area. I placed my packages on the conveyer belt that passed the items through the x-ray machine. The female security guard stopped the belt and told me to open one of my bags. It was the one containing the hefty jewelry. They were large jeweled necklaces that were mounted on heavy metal. It was understandable to me why the machine would flag the weighty, jewelry-encrusted metal. After the necklaces and bracelets were inspected, I was told to go. As I picked up my plastic bags which had passed through on the conveyer belt, it seemed I had fewer bags than when I entered. I asked the security guard sitting behind the screen of the machine if I had all my bags. She told me, "Yes, that is everything." I stood there and indicated that I had more bags that entered the machine than had exited. The guard rudely insisted that I leave. I didn't, and insisted I was missing a bag. Again, she loudly directed me to leave. I leaned over, parted the vertical straps, and looked at the belt inside the machine. As I did, I thought I saw another package which I felt was mine. The guard noisily and offensively bellowed for me not to touch the machine. I told her I thought I saw my other package of gifts still in the machine. She again yelled there was nothing in the machine. She specified she was looking at her screen and saw nothing. As a result of the shaming and bully tactics, and doubting my memory, I unwillingly picked up my three bags. I was thinking I was possibly mistaken and turned to leave the security area to return to my cabin.

With my back to the security conveyer belt, I had to wait for a large group of passengers passing through a narrow opening to leave the ship. It may have been a wait of several minutes. I was still feeling that a bag of mine was missing. When I returned to my cabin, I planned to lay all the items on my bed and see if I could remember if anything was missing. I couldn't check my receipts because they were in the packages with the gifts. If a bag was missing, so too would be the receipt. As the last of the departing guests leaving the ship passed through the narrow opening, and I was about to leave the security area, I heard a male voice call out to me. I turned and saw a security guard holding up a plastic bag. This was the bag I thought I had all along. I walked back to the conveyer belt machine and retrieved my bag. As I did, I expected an apology from the rude female guard, but none came. Even though I was a few feet from her, she never even looked at me.

I had never been treated rudely before while aboard a cruise ship and was disturbed by the incident. I then thought the guard could have been doing this act many times before, and may have been a clever thief. When back in my room, I called the purser and reported the unpleasant incident. I wanted the ship's management to be aware of a possible scam run by their security personnel.

About two hours later a received a phone call from "James." He identified himself as the head of security. I explained the incident to him and detailed the rudeness of the guard. He asked me to describe her. I told him she wore a white officer's uniform, was Indian, and was short and fat. He abruptly told me he knew exactly to whom I was referring. He indicated he would handle it. He sounded angry when he realized who I was describing. I believe he recognized the woman's behavior from a previous experience. I never heard from James or the purser regarding this incident again. I wish I had. I at least should have been offered an apology. Other cruise lines, when passengers were treated rudely by employees, would send a gift, like a bottle of wine, to the passenger. I received nothing from *Dark Ship's* management.

The date was March 20th, and I had another four weeks remaining on the cruise. I passed through the security system on numerous additional occasions. I never again saw the short, fat, female guard. I assume she was fired—maybe even arrested. I imagined her cabin and belongings were searched and a stash of contraband was found. I believed it was very possible she was a criminal, but I was never given any information in that regard. I only know I never saw her again.

Chapter 9

COMMUNICATION CONFUSION

Whether one is running a ship, a military unit, or a vast corporation, proper communication must be passed down to the subordinates from the commanding general, the CEO, management, or whatever the boss is called. This insures the proper functioning of the unit.

Aboard *Dark Ship*, it was annoyingly noticeable that something was lacking. A prime example of this mismanagement was the lack of communication. As an example, I offer the confusion that reigned regarding the gala dinner of the world cruise passengers. It was in Dubai at a six-star hotel. The grounds were magnificent. The hotel structure was glorious, both its interior and exterior. Tasteful art exhibits and beautiful landscape design abounded.

Unfortunately, the notification to the passengers attending was disastrous. Using myself as an example, on the day of the event, I had to contact the purser to ask the following questions:

1. What time is the event?
2. Where do we meet the busses?
3. When do we meet the busses?
4. What is the dress code?
5. What is my table number?

The purser told me all the information was explained in the letter. I responded by asking, "When will the letter be delivered to me?" I was told it was delivered to me several days ago. I explained that I never received any letter. I was told to contact the world cruise concierge.

I called the world cruise concierge and was told the answers to my questions were explained in the letter. I asked, "When will the letter be delivered to me?" I was told it was sent several days ago. I explained I never received a letter. I again was told the letter was sent to me. I responded, "I never received any letter regarding the world cruise dinner." I was again told that it was sent to me. I then, somewhat annoyed now, asked where I could go to get the letter. And yet again, I was reminded that a letter was sent to me. I then, openly annoyed, reminded the woman that I was constantly left off the receiving end of many letters. I never received an invitation to the captain's reception for solo travelers. I never received an invitation to the captain's reception for world cruise passengers. And I never received an invitation to the captain's reception for diamond member passengers. I am a member of each of these groups, but never had the invitations delivered to me. I found out about these events from my tablemates. I also found out that I wasn't the only one who failed to receive various letters, notifications, and invitations.

One topic of conversation among my tablemates was whether it was a lack of management to oversee the tasks assigned or just incompetence on many levels. I am convinced it was a lack of management.

Another area where inadequate communication is evident is the *TV Guide*. Most passengers watch the TV as part of their daily routine. The *TV Guide* is almost always incorrect. A new *TV Guide* is issued at the beginning of each segment of the voyage. Sometimes there is no *TV Guide* for the first few days of each voyage segment. Newly embarked passengers who have never sailed before spend most of the first day scrolling through the channels trying to find a program to watch. When they do receive a guide indicating the channel numbers and programs, they become exasperated to discover that the programs, times, and channels hardly ever match up. I wondered if the person who made up the *TV Guide* did so in a time zone and the times would be good for that location only. Could it be possible that he paid no attention as to where the ship would be on the globe where the time is different? If so, then what would account for the channel mix-up? The intermixing of shows and channels could only be the fault of the writer of the program and the managing editor. Again, *Dark Ship's* lack of management was evident.

Another management disaster is the distribution of the Daily Program and the Newsletter. The Daily Program is a listing of all the events of the day, the times, location of events, and teachers. This program brochure, when things run right, is delivered to the cabin the night before. This way passengers can make plans for events during the upcoming day. It is an annoyance when the Daily Program is not delivered the night before, because the passengers are unable to prepare for events of the next day.

Another annoyance occurs when changes are made to previously indicated events. An example of this is when I booked an excursion to an interesting Arab country. The booking ticket indicated we would meet in the theater at 0930. A week prior to the trip, a letter was sent to me indicating the meeting time was changed to 0900. Two days before the event, another letter was delivered to me changing the time to 0830. On the morning of the excursion, I decided to go to the theater to meet the group at 0815, which was fifteen minutes early. When I arrived, I saw the leader, with a pole in the air, leaving the theater with a long line from my group following her. Had I not decided to go fifteen minutes early, I would have missed the departing group, missed the trip, and lost the money I paid for the trip.

As previously mentioned in this chapter, communication is necessary for the proper direction of an entity. When visiting a port, guests either travel independently or with a ship's planned excursion. When an excursion is booked through the ship, the tour company is responsible for delivering the passengers back to the ship in time for the scheduled sailing. When traveling independently, the passenger, either renting or sharing a private car, is responsible for returning at the indicated time. If he is unable to make it back on time, it is helpful to call the ship and report it so the ship can come to rescue the passenger or make arrangements to delay the sailing.

Whenever visiting a port, the ship prints a map of the city for the convenience of those passengers who wish to visit the port on their own. The guest who chooses to travel on his own, and not with a ship-sponsored tour, finds the map to be helpful in finding his way to interesting sites. In addition, the map is a convenience in finding one's way back to the ship when traveling on foot.

The map is something that is never forgotten when leaving the ship to visit the port. In the event of an emergency, it would be convenient if the ship's emergency phone number was placed on the map. It is not on the map, but on the Daily Program. Thankfully, I never needed the emergency phone number. I often thought if I did need that number, it was back in my cabin. The map, which I always had with me, had no phone number on it. The Daily Program, which I never thought to bring along, had the number on it, which did me no good because it was in my cabin. Gee, why not print the number on the map?

Duh! What is wrong with the communications on this ship? There was obviously another change made of this excursion, and I was, again, left out of the loop.

Regarding the Daily Program, information on the shuttle bus was clearly visible on a beautiful sunny February day in port. It explained the hours of shuttle bus operation. It explained where to meet the bus at the cruise terminal in Shanghai. It also explained, in detail, where the bus would allow passengers to depart in the city center of Shanghai. It was a perfect location for the bus to shuttle the passengers to. It was at a park on a river with shopping and vendors nearby. The park on the river was magnificent.

Now, one would wonder why Shanghai's information is chronicled in a space designed by the author for *Dark Ship's* mismanagement and misinformation. Well, it is because we were not in Shanghai. We were in Tianjin! It was information for a port we were in several days earlier.

Chalk up another failure for *Dark Ship*.

Chapter 10

Dark Ship's Worst Day

Although most days on *Dark Ship* were disorganized, the day we tendered into Penang, Malaysia, was an abominable horror show. To tender in means the ship is unable to tie up to a solidly constructed dock. Tendering means one must step off a large rocking ship onto a small, fifty-passenger lifeboat that doubles as a tender. Passengers are crowded onto small bench seats for the ride into shore. The tenders always rock significantly more than the ship. Some people will not ride in a tender or book an excursion due to motion sickness. Others will not tender due to the danger of transferring oneself from the ship to the rocking, smaller boat. Still others, with health or mobility difficulties, are prevented from boarding the tenders due to the possibility of injury. The ship's rules prevent anyone from boarding the tender if they have any ambulatory issues. Anyone spotted with a cane is made to take a quick mobility test before being allowed to board a tender.

I was on a cruise when a crew member was killed by falling into the water between the ship and the tender. The poor man was crushed. The ship's staff take the safety aspect of tendering very seriously. There are two crew members positioned on the entrance to the tender. They assist all passengers in the boarding of the boat. Each crew member grabs the passenger who is boarding the tender firmly under each arm for safety. You are told only to step on the boat when it is rising. The boat is much smaller than the ship and drastically rises and falls, presenting a danger to boarding passengers. Debarking the tender at dockside is never as threatening because the dock is not moving, although two crew members are still positioned there to assist. In addition, the seas are calmer at the shoreside dock because it is always located in a safe harbor.

At Penang, thankfully there were no incidents debarking the ship in the morning. Returning to the ship in the afternoon was a completely different story.

After attending a tour on this day, the passengers on my bus and I returned to the cruise terminal in Penang. I was not aware of any problem until I departed the escalator to the second floor of the terminal. As the escalator reached the top of its passage and I attempted to step off, I was greeted by a wall of humanity and was unable to alight from the escalator. I stood motionless for a moment because I could not proceed further due to huge numbers of people standing around and blocking the exit. An instant later I was pushed with great force by passengers rising on the escalator behind me. Not understanding what was occurring, I wormed my way through the crowd to get away from the dangerous escalator. Amid the confusion and commotion, I soon understood what was happening. There were people being fed into the terminal, but no one was leaving. I heard people shouting at newly arrived passengers coming up the escalator to get at the end of the queue (a British term for line). The line wound around the huge terminal, which was larger than a football field. There was no order to the line. It wound around like an unsystematic snake. I found a safe place away from the dangerous escalator which was near the closed exit to the tenders. All those around me were confused and disturbed by the commotion around us. There soon appeared two white uniformed officers from the ship, apologizing for the delay. They made no attempt to organize the line, but just allowed the shouting and commotion to continue. The two officers merely offered their apologies. They gave no direction nor an explanation for the anger and disastrous confusion in the Penang Cruise Terminal.

It turns out the tender operation was halted for two and a half hours. As passengers arrived at the cruise terminal from their shore excursions, they were given no direction and just allowed to disorderly mingle in a disorganized line with thousands of confused people.

The reason for the delay varied according to whom you spoke. One excuse given was that we had to wait for a ferry to pass. Ferries, we were told, took precedence over tenders. This could not be true because a passing ferry would take no more than ten minutes. We accepted this as a plain lie.

The other reason given for the delay was that the seas were too rough. None of us could recognize the seas as any rougher than when we came ashore in the morning. This too had to be a lie.

So, what was the real reason? A harbor workers' strike holding the ship hostage until they paid the newly imposed fee? A rumor circulated that the local government demanded more money from the cruise line. It was alleged that the ransom was paid, and the delay occurred while waiting for the payment to clear the bank deposit. I'm leaning toward accepting something along those lines as the reason. Or else, why the obvious lies? Lies are bred from guilt, and the cruise line surely smelled of guilt.

Whatever the reason, *Dark Ship's* leadership should have sent officers ashore to organize the lines in the terminal. Passengers left alone to deal with an emergency such as existed is pure negligence. White-suited officers and ship's personnel should have been mobilized and sent to the terminal to maintain order. There was a distinct need for an authority figure to organize the queues.

After a three-hour shutdown, the doors were opened, the line moved forward, and we began to board the tenders. No explanation was given—not at that time, or at any time, by the captain or any of the ship's personnel. The next day's noon report by the captain to the ship's passengers was noticeably devoid of any explanation.

At this point, I must mention the captain's noon report to the ship was always late. It was rumored that there was a lottery, betting on how long after noon the report would be given, organized by the passengers. Many passengers felt that the captain was so disorganized, he couldn't get his report made on time. This proved to them that he bore the blame for all the disorganization.

With all the disruption that occurred at the cruise terminal, easily forgotten was the beauty of the butterfly garden we visited in Penang.

Chapter 11

SINGAPORE

The overnight visit to Singapore was a pleasant one. The first day, I went on an excursion called "Breakfast in the Wild." We left the ship very early and arrived at the Singapore Zoo. There was a buffet breakfast waiting for us. The foods offered were mostly Asian and unlike any I ever tasted. They were delightful. There was a juice like nothing I had ever tasted. I believe it must have been a mixture of several juices. I enjoyed it. I also had an egg mix that included mystery meats and vegetables. I enjoyed that too. I didn't have the breads and pancake-like entrees because I decided to go back to my gluten-free diet. I thought I was over my gluten intolerance, but again began to suffer the gluten-caused symptoms of dermatitis herpetiformis. A biopsy I had ten years ago indicated I suffered from this autoimmune disease. I thought I was over it, but obviously not so. The disease causes itchy rashes all over my body. Thankfully, it is annoying but not life-threatening.

After breakfast, the tour guide cut us loose for a few hours, giving us a meeting place where we could board the bus back to the ship.

At the well-planned and amply stocked zoo, I saw primates, a rare white tiger, and a beautiful blue-crowned pigeon. Each of these I was able to capture in interesting photographs.

It was a zoo designed in the new manner of replicating the habitat and environment of the species' natural environments. I enjoyed the visit, and it provided many photo opportunities.

The ship had an overnight stay in Singapore. My next day's excursion was to the awesome Marina Bay Mall. The cruise line provided a shuttle bus, and I utilized it, allowing me to enjoy the day.

Chapter 12

Travel Companions

The finest experiences I had on the cruise aboard *Dark Ship* were with the passengers. As on my previous cruises, I rarely met a person I didn't like. Most people were enjoyable, but some were fascinating.

One man I became friends with was Stanley Hartmann. He was a superhero type who had been a world traveler for the last forty years. In the 1980s, he became a millionaire at the age of twenty-two. It was during the infancy of the technological revolution when he developed a software company. He created the ability to enhance the organizing of computer files. He sold it to a megacompany for many millions, and his life suddenly became interesting.

Stanley, who was a dashing Indiana Jones type of character, majored in archeology in college. As a young man, he decided to mount an expedition to the Amazon River region, looking for an ancient culture. He used all the millions he received from the sale of his computer company to outfit his project. The area to be explored was in Brazil, deep in the heart of the Amazon. Stanley used old maps and notes from the early Portuguese explorers, who indicated there was a lost city of gold. Stanley thought he would use his freshly made millions to discover treasures and secrets of the ancient world. He was certain he would achieve fame and fortune from this venture. He was shocked when he set ashore in Santorum, Brazil, and found all his equipment confiscated by the government. It seems the area he was going to enter was inhabited by secretive indigenous people protected by the government, and no part of the outside world was permitted to encounter them due to the fear of global diseases that the tribe had no immunity to. Based on past experiences, the Brazilian government found that entire tribes would die from the common diseases to which the modern world had developed resistance.

Stanley left the United States a millionaire bent on world fame and returned penniless. He was a poorer but wiser man. He published his experiences as a biographic, nonfiction, literal work. He was hopeful he would recoup some of his losses. The book was quickly purchased by Stanley's family and larger group of friends. The initial sales gave Stanley confidence, which lasted for the first month. Then all sales dropped off and it sold a total of one hundred and eighty copies to the rest of the world. Stanley, with a wealth of research material, notes on his travel, and his daily log, set about writing a novel. His story idea was so intriguing, and the subject was so interesting, the book became an instant best seller. In addition, Hollywood saw a hit movie and purchased the story from Stanley.

Stanley, with his royalties from book sales and the contract from Hollywood, was back to living a comfortable life. The first thing he did was to book a world cruise.

Stanley liked to consume alcohol. He liked it more when his alcohol consumption was in the company of others. His favorite time was when he consumed alcohol in the company of women. His motto was "Candy is dandy, but liquor is quicker." This was in reference to getting women to accompany him to his cabin. The only time it was inconvenient for a lady to come to Stanley's cabin was when he was sharing it with another woman. This was due to his occasionally taking a lady friend to accompany him on a segment of the cruise. He regarded the trip as an extended date.

I met Stanley at a solo travelers meeting one day. He was a cheerful man with a rosy, cherub-like, friendly face. He was speaking to a woman he introduced as Mandy. She was younger than most of the other solo travelers and quite attractive. She said she was a newly retired elementary schoolteacher from Chicago. She made pleasant conversation regarding her travels throughout the United States. She traveled during the summer months when she was on summer vacation from her teaching job. She loved the Rocky Mountain states, and was particularly familiar with South Park, Colorado. She described it as a huge plateau that lay between the front range of Colorado and the Collegiate Range, which ran from north to south down the western section of the United States. Mandy raved about the pure air and high altitude. She said it was a pleasant departure from the humidity of her Chicago home.

Mandy indicated she was recently disabled from an automobile accident. She explained that she was in a coma for a week as a result of a head injury. Hearing this, I realized how someone so young—she looked to be in her forties—could be retired and afford a luxury cruise. I soon realized the extent of her condition because, as we were leaving, she became excited and looked all around for her eyeglasses. She got on her hands and knees to look under tables and along the carpeted floor. Several of us immediately assisted, looking all around the area she sat in. The commotion ended when someone exclaimed, "Mandy, you are wearing them."

Noticeably embarrassed, Mandy apologized profusely.

She then loudly asked the group, "Whose lipstick is this?" as she held the article in the air.

"Where did it come from?" someone asked.

"Right here," she responded, "in my purse."

Now realizing Mandy's disability was so profound, everyone was kind and helpful, trying to assist her in her plight. "Are you sure that is your purse?" someone delicately asked.

"Oh my God, I hope I didn't pick up the wrong purse again." She checked inside and found it was her purse because her room key card was in there.

As we left, we felt bad for her because the group determined the lipstick in question was Mandy's after all. She just didn't recognize it.

As we were leaving the restaurant where the solo traveler coffee was held, Stanley told me he was planning to have a fling with Mandy, but after seeing the mental condition she was in, decided against it.

At breakfast the next morning, Stan indicated he was presently sharing his cabin with an older German woman he met on a previous cruise. He said she retired early in the evening. After she fell asleep, he would go out to frequent the shipboard night spots to meet other women. If they were solo travelers, it would suit his needs because the sleeping Inga prevented him from bringing a woman to his cabin.

He told the story of his previous cruise when an angry English husband head-butted him and broke his nose. When I inquired as to the circumstances, he said that while he was in the after-hours disco, a drunk woman approached him and sat on his lap. She straddled him in his chair, wrapped both arms around him, and kissed him on his neck. Her name was Margaret; she was in her thirties, and significantly drunk. Embarrassed, Stanley politely tried to pry her off and remove her from his lap. He thought it would be prudent to dance with her rather than having a woman draped all over him. He was just as uncomfortable dancing with her because he had to hold her against himself to prevent her from falling to the dance floor.

It seems the woman had just had an argument with her husband and told him she wanted a divorce. The husband entered the disco and saw his wife draped over Stanley. He flew into a rage and pulled his wife away, causing her to fall to the floor. When Stanley questioned his act, he was promptly head-butted in the face. Security was called, and the video footage was checked. Stanley was led to the infirmary, and the husband was banished to his cabin and ordered off the ship at the next port.

Stanley never saw the woman again, although he often wondered what she would be like in bed.

Stanley soon led into a sexual experience he had which he referred to as "the Asian mix-up." It seems on one of his cruises, he developed an intimate relationship with a Japanese woman. They spent a delightful romance for a week while on a Mediterranean cruise. When they parted in Venice, they exchanged phone numbers, addresses, and emails. They swore they would remain in contact and if ever in each other's countries would surely contact one another. Travelers who meet on cruises always promise to remain in touch, but this usually amounts to just a few back-and-forth emails, if that.

Much to Stanley's surprise, he received a call from a Japanese woman he exchanged emails with. He was delighted when she took him up on his offer to stay at his sprawling home in Atlanta, Georgia. He picked her up at the airport and drove her to his home in a posh neighborhood. Remembering his intimacy with her, he carried her luggage straight to his bedroom.

They spent a wonderful night together. In the morning, he prepared a huge Southern breakfast.

The woman told him at breakfast that she was surprised when he took her luggage to his bedroom. She was delighted, however, at the thought. It was then that Stanley realized this was not the Japanese woman with whom he previously shared an intimacy. This was a different Japanese woman. He merely met her casually on board a cruise, and she was one of many he offered an invitation to visit him and tour the American South.

As he related the story of the Asian mix-up, I could see fond memories of the incident reflecting in his eyes.

Another interesting story Stanley told was from the German woman who stayed with him for a segment of the cruise.

She told of an incident that occurred when she was a young girl. During a certain time of the year when the weather was right, her family would go into the woods near her home to search for mushrooms. Her father would then prepare them and serve them for Sunday dinner. It took an experienced person to know the look of poisonous mushrooms so they could be avoided. On one particular Sunday after the well-prepared meal, she noticed her cat, who consumed the leftovers, was acting strangely. Her mother immediately thought that some of the mushrooms were of the poisonous type. "Hans, how could you be so stupid. You have poisoned us all."

Her father replied, "I am certain we only picked the safe mushrooms."

"No," said her mother, "you are so stupid, you have killed us all." They all observed the cat noisily rolling on the floor and in pain. "You see, she is dying. I knew they tasted differently," Mother snapped.

Her father, feeling he may have allowed some bad mushrooms into the pile they had eaten, quickly packed everyone off to the hospital. Although no one felt ill, her mother said that the cat's digestive system worked more rapidly than humans and was an indication that the mushrooms were poisonous. At the hospital, the medical staff agreed that each of their stomachs had to be pumped out. This was a procedure that the entire family suffered with great discomfort. As they were driving home, they all were certain that their beloved pet cat would be dead. Her father, feeling guilt and shame, apologized several times. They were all saddened by the thought of their beloved Minnie, an excellent mouser, being dead. Her mother said, "Now we will have to get another cat immediately or we will be overrun with mice. All because you couldn't tell the poisonous mushrooms from the edible ones."

Upon arriving at home they were anxious to see the condition Minnie was in. They had to search for her because she was not in her usual place of comfort, the kitchen. They heard her call from the master bedroom. Much to everyone's surprise, she was in the dark closet. When they opened the door and looked down at the scene, they were startled by the sight. Staring up at them, meowing with pride, in her orange and white coat, was a very healthy Minnie, who greeted them with a soft meow. Cuddled next to her were five furry kittens.

It seems the mushrooms were of the safe species after all.

Chapter 13

BILL O'NEILL'S STORIES

A memorable experience occurred when Bill, a retired fire chief, explained his duties while employed by the New York City Fire Department. He told two fascinating stories of incidents he encountered while at work.

He was returning from a call early one Sunday morning in Brooklyn with his fire company. He hopped off his truck to direct the driver backing into the firehouse when he heard a frantic call for help from the alley next to their building. He ran to investigate and noticed a nude woman hanging out a window of the building next to the firehouse. He ordered two men to get the ladder, and they ran down the alley to place it next to the frantic woman. The men immediately began to argue who would climb the ladder to save the nude victim. Bill had to quickly decide which of the two eager men would climb the ladder to rescue the naked woman. The woman continued her frantic screams, indicating there was a murderer in her apartment. Bill had to make a quick command decision: seniority would be the deciding factor. The junior man had the responsibility of butting the ladder; that is, to hold it firmly with his foot on the bottom rung to prevent slippage. It would be the senior man who would have the dangerous but desirable job of rescuing the attractive, stark-naked woman.

By now the entire company was gathered under the still screaming, terrified, unclothed woman. As the senior man climbed the ladder, he situated himself next to and a little below the woman. He then told her to swing her leg over to his direction where he could grasp it. His intention was to have her place her foot on the rung of the ladder located at his shoulder. In her panic, she chose the stability of her rescuer's body to cling to. Because he was below the woman, her leg went over his shoulder, and he had to use his great strength to stabilize the frightened woman. It was a comical scene because, until the fireman could talk the woman into placing her feet on the rungs of the ladder, his head was trapped between her thighs. The nude victim felt secure now because she had both hands off the windowsill and firmly planted on the rungs of the ladder. As the firemen tried to talk her into releasing the fireman's head, she continued her screaming. Due to her panic and fear, she refused to release him. It seems while making her transfer from the windowsill to the rescuing, there were a few moments where she had both her legs dangling over her rescuer's back with his face buried in her crotch. Fortunately, the senior fireman did not lack for advice from below as to how to maneuver the screaming, nude woman. Suggestions were continually shouted up from the firemen gathered at the base of the ladder. They explained to her how to lean on one thigh against the rescuer's shoulder and twist in the same direction. The senior fireman was relieved at this point because as she released her grip from his face, he was now able to catch a breath. He was now confident he would not die of asphyxiation from two thighs squeezing his ears and nose and mouth, crushed against her panicked body. She was finally able to turn her body so she was sitting on his shoulders facing the same way as he. They were then able to awkwardly descend the ladder.

When they reached the bottom, there was no lack of volunteers to assist in getting the panicked woman off her rescuer.

Then the police arrived, which is expected when a nude woman claims she escaped a rapist/murderer. The New York Police Department quickly solved the crime and made arrests the next day.

It seems the woman, no longer nude and garbed in firemen's work clothes, felt she was in need of emotional support and was allowed to phone her pastor. She often went to him for spiritual comfort. As the phone was answered, the woman's face turned ashen. This alarmed the lead detective, observing with great interest the victim's fearful behavior. Holding the phone away from her face, she whispered this was the voice of the man who raped and attempted to kill her. The detective, who was sitting next to her, quickly took the phone, and using a ruse, was able to get the man's identity and arrange a meeting.

It seems the pastor had a sexual relationship with the victim and was angered when she broke off the relationship. The pastor offered the church's handyman a payment of all he could steal from the woman, as he knew she had a goodly number of valuables. In addition, he was told, before killing her he could rape her. The valuables included savings bonds and jewelry. The handyman was told exactly where the valuables were hidden. He agreed and the murder plan was put into effect. The woman was tricked into opening her apartment door and the violence began. The pastor's henchman, using the threat of his knife, had her undress and submit to him. After the rape, as the man was retrieving his knife, the victim realized what was to be her fate. She distracted the killer by telling him where the jewels were hidden. When he left the room, she quickly locked herself in her bedroom, climbed out her window, and screamed as loudly as she could. It was her good fortune that the fire engines had arrived at that time.

The police detectives questioned the handyman, who, realizing the trouble he was in, immediately implicated the pastor. The handyman had done this twice before for the pastor and was told he was blessed by God for his actions because he was killing the devil's followers.

Two criminals were behind bars with two murders solved. One senior fireman would forever be remembered for his heroic ladder rescue. One handyman would cry and call to Jesus, saying that he just followed the directions of a man of God. One pastor claimed he was set up by the forces of the devil, and only wanted to help the two women he had murdered. He insisted he was a good man and Jesus had forgiven him.

We finished our steak dinners in the specialty restaurant as we listened with great interest to Bill's firehouse story. Cindy, one of our group, asked if Bill had any other memorable moments during his career as a New York City firefighter. As we sat in the restaurant, the six of us listened with great interest to Bill's next story.

It seems one Christmas season there was a bad fire in a tenement on the lower east side of New York City. Bill and another firefighter were assigned to check if any residents were left in the building. As they were climbing the smoke-filled stairs, they heard a woman's screams, calling for help. The panicked woman said her sister was an invalid and she needed help carrying her out. Bill, a large powerful man, told his partner to take the first woman down and he would carry out the disabled woman. At this time a loudspeaker from the fire truck in the street announced there was a fire in the building and all residents must exit. The disabled sister in a front room heard the announcement and immediately leaped from the bed and ran for the apartment's exit.

Seeing this, the first sister, who refused to leave without her "disabled" sister, immediately realized her sibling was not disabled at all. Perceiving her fearfully running sister, she screamed, "You muthafuckin lying bitch. You made me serve you hand and foot for three years. I let you live with me, I fed you, I took you for visits to the doctor. You lying muthafuckin bitch, all these years you was fuckin with me. Lordy, Lordy, you gotta punish her ass."

"Oh my God," the other fireman declared. "She can walk. It must a Christmas miracle."

The Story of Lois Broomfield

I met Lois on the final leg of my world cruise—the Atlantic crossing from England to New York. She showed up at the dinner table containing five of us regulars and three new diners. The three newbies were a stuffy British man; Lois, a lesbian New Yorker who called Germany her home for the last few years; and a person who never appeared for dinner. We were never sure if the absent diner was a male or female.

Upon our initial introductions, Reginald, the British man, observing Lois' wedding band and asked where her husband was. Lois answered, "My wife is in Germany and I am going on a three-week vacation to visit her American friends and family." At the mentioning of her wife, I instantly knew Lois was proudly declaring herself a lesbian. The Brit, not picking up on her answer, wanted to know why she was traveling without her husband. She replied that *she* was a CEO of a large corporation and was unable to get away at that time. Reginald still didn't get the "she" description of her partner.

Lois is an attractive, energetic, and entertaining person. She is a former script writer for Americans sitcoms. In addition, she toured worldwide performing as a standup comedienne. One of the interesting stories she told was regarding her ability to speak fractured German. She said she never had formal language classes in German but just picked it up in her travels and her residency in Frankfurt.

She told of her German neighbors who accepted her and her partner's lifestyle. She then related a story of dealing with a neighbor who had an annoying barking dog. She paid him a visit and told him in German that his dog was an annoyance and that he should feed his dog. The man immediately showed his anger by responding in a verbal tirade. Not understanding a word he said, but realizing his response was significantly unfriendly, she sought help from her partner to interpret what the neighbor said to her. It was settled in a friendly manner when the neighbor was made to realize this American woman wanted to tell him to feed your dog, not eat your dog.

I found Lois to be the most delightful friend I made on my world cruise.

Mindy Crawford

Mindy, a retired nurse, was a passenger on the world cruise who sat at our dinner table. She was an energetic person, often flashing a smile. She was noted for having the most suggestions for what and where to visit whenever we were in a port. In addition, she was known for being overly concerned with the condition of the dinner table. Mindy particularly was concerned with the condition of the fresh flowers. If they were not fresh, she would be quick to make her displeasure known and request new flowers. She always tended the flowers by nipping off the dead leaves or flowers when she thought the action was essential.

Another aspect of her obsessive behavior was made evident by her reprimanding anyone who fiddled with their silverware while waiting for the meals to be delivered by the waiters. The most annoying behavior Mindy displayed, though, was the seating of the diners. She was unhappy unless the other diners were seated boy, girl, boy, girl, etc. When there wasn't an even number of males and females, she wanted the seating to be according to her choice. Needless to say, not everyone complied with her wishes.

On one occasion, when Mindy insisted the table members shift seats to accommodate her obsessive-compulsive behavior, some table members refused to comply. It was plain to see she was not going to give up on her demands that two people change their seats. The impasse was broken by a quip made by one of the group. He declared, "This is a dinner group, not an orgy." Everyone laughed and the uneasiness of the moment passed.

Ruth Crowder

One of the nicer memories that remains with me is of Ruth, a retired Scotland Yard sergeant. She was a youthful blonde, about five feet, eight inches tall, who possessed a svelte body. She had a second-degree black belt in the Tai Kwon Do form of karate. When asked of her duties at Scotland Yard, she was elusive. "Oh, nothing that would be considered out of the ordinary." No matter how much she downplayed her importance, the belief was that she worked at a covert position of great importance.

I had the distinct pleasure of sharing two excursions with Ruth. One of the trips, to a zoo in Malaysia, was pleasantly memorable. We had breakfast together and spent three pleasant hours roaming through interesting zoological displays. In that time I appeased my curiosity by asking her what she did as a Scotland Yard officer. She told me it wasn't office work. It seems she spent time in restaurants and lounges targeting known criminals and evildoers. She hoped to get them relaxed with drink and get them talking about their illegal activities. Ruth indicated she always had backup and wore a listening device, so she was never in much danger. When I asked about her work, Ruth was, at first, evasive and not eager to reveal her background. In pleasant conversation during the day, we realized we both had training in Tai Kwon Do. That was what led me to believe her area of work specialty was of a dangerous nature.

As the interesting day wore on at the zoo, I noticed she scrutinized the other zoo visitors. It gave me the feeling that she was conducting a threat assessment of all who passed us. When I asked her about it, she indicated she learned that from her job and old habits die hard.

While we walked the length and breadth of the zoo's grounds, she finally loosened up and shared some of her work-related experiences with me.

It seems, as she targeted bars, restaurants, and lounges, she met many disreputable characters. One of them she described was a leader of a gang that dealt in stolen cars. It became evident that his crew was part of an international ring that targeted luxury cars and would take them from the streets. The man she pursued was in charge of shipping the cars to various South American ports. Other elements of the ring existed that indicated the vastness of the operation. There also was a unit that changed the vehicle identification numbers and then moved the cars to where they were loaded into containers and transported to the container facility at the shipyard. At the beginning of the robbery chain was the crew that identified the car itself. This was at the level of the auto sales lot and at automobile servicing shops. Ruth was responsible for the bringing down of a huge auto theft operation that operated throughout Europe. Never before did Interpol or Scotland Yard comprehend the vastness of the auto theft operation. There was the initial targeting of the car by one unit. Then there was the sweeping it up from the street by another crew who were skilled car thieves. After that, the body shop enacted the changing of the color and identity of the auto. It was usually stored at a different location. This operation was followed by packing the stolen vehicle into a container and, finally, loading it on the ships for transportation to South America.

Ruth was a hero, but she couldn't ever be identified as such because she worked undercover. I was proud to know her.

Chapter 14

UNFORGETTABLE MOMENTS HATEFUL HAMID

A haunting incident occurred on a tour in Aqaba, Jordan. I loved the movie *Lawrence of Arabia*. I remembered one of the battle scenes was filmed on location in Aqaba, at Wadi Rum. I quickly signed up for that tour, and because many tours were sold out, I was pleased to get it.

The most unforgettable part of this excursion was the hatred and anger exhibited by the tour guide. He was an older man in his sixties who introduced himself as Hamid. He said he was a college professor and had been doing tours for twenty-two years. After the tour bus was loaded with passengers, someone asked him if the city visible across the Gulf of Aqaba was Eilat, Israel. That question, at the very beginning of the tour, set Hamid off on a tirade. He, displaying significant anger, went on to harangue the existence of Israel. He then said he was a college professor. By identifying himself as a professor, he was indicating that his beliefs should go unchallenged. He said that Israel should not be allowed to exist because it was illegal. With great emotion, he went on to say that Israelis kill Palestinian children every day. "Check the newspapers if you don't believe me," he said. "You can see the proof that the Israelis are murderers of Palestinian children. It is right there for you to read. Every day, it's there, just read it." He continued his diatribe. "There would be no Israel if it weren't for you British. That's right, you British are the cause. In 1948, you…" and at this point he paused and stared into the faces of many of the riders on the bus, "were the cause of the problems of today. We were a peaceful Palestine until 1948. We were Palestine from the beginning of time, but you British decided to cause this problem." For twenty minutes Hamid continued his angry scolding. I remember reading of terrorists who took over an establishment and would harangue their hostages before they killed them. I began to fear that this tour wasn't going to end well.

Strangely, when we entered the port in Jordan, the satellite news feed was cut off from our television monitors aboard the ship. All other programs worked well, but CNN, Fox News, Sky News, MSNBC, and other news stations were mysteriously blacked out. The news stations resumed their normal function as we departed from Jordan. I didn't think much of it then, but now believe that may be part of the agreement the cruise line made in order to be allowed to enter their country. I don't know this for a fact, but believe it is logical.

The frightening twenty minutes of verbal abuse ended when Hamid changed the subject and became engrossed in the description of the Seven Pillars of Wisdom, the site we were on our way to visit.

As we approached the parking lot, Hamid told us of the several shopping stalls and the wonderful gifts we could purchase. He then said to be back at the bus in thirty minutes. As I departed the bus and headed toward the viewing site, I realized that to get to the site for good photographs, I would have little time to visit the shops because of the long distance and the maneuvering through the thick crowd of visitors. After rushing through the photographs and heading back to the bus and vendors, I could hear Hamid's voice loudly calling, "Bus three, bus number three, bus three, over here." I realized that was my bus and barely had time to get back to it. I then looked at my watch and realized the thirty-minute time period was not nearly used up. In fact, only fifteen minutes had passed. It seemed to me that Hamid was either a control freak or didn't care a bit for his countrymen's livelihood, the vendors. That time would have been happily spent browsing the shops laden with interesting native items.

After visiting a Bedouin village for lunch, which was quite enjoyable, we headed back to the ship, where the guide gave the usual "Don't forget the driver and how much you enjoyed the tour" as an appeal for tips. At this point the passengers, who are usually pleased with their guide, will applaud. On this tour a mere few people gave a mild applause. Hamid then loudly exclaimed, "Don't give us clapping. We can't take it to the store to buy food.

Dig into your pockets and give us money. I will be at the door to remind you if you forget." I could immediately see passengers looking over their shoulders to spot the rear door where they could exit and avoid the horrible Hamid. Hamid, who had twenty-two years' experience, by his own admission, made sure the rear door was not open for the departing passengers. All passengers had to exit the vehicle and face the Hateful Hamid.

The departure from the bus was slower than usual because Hamid was intimidating the departing passengers into digging through their pockets or purses for a tip. True to his word, Hamid stood directly in front of the bus exit and had his hand out for his tip. I stepped off and was nose to nose with the disagreeable Hamid and declared, "I really enjoyed lunch." He was so close to me, I had to brush him with my shoulder to get past him and return to the ship. I always give a tip to the tour guides who are always friendly and wonderful ambassadors for their country. The act of omitting a tip to this angry, beastly man was upsetting for me. In the past, I always left a tour feeling good with my two-Euro tip in my hand, but not this time. It was also the first time I promised myself I would notify the tour office and purser of the intimidating actions of Hateful Hamid.

The purser indicated to me that he would report this man to the Jordanian tour company who employs him. The next day the purser called me and issued an apology for the behavior of the hateful Hamid. I responded that I wanted an apology from the tour company who employed Hamid. I indicated I would not be pleased until I received that apology. I never received it, nor did I hear of the incident again.

Chapter 15

ELEGANT DINING

The appearance and design of the main restaurant on *Dark Ship* were superb. The walnut and mahogany walls with pleasant molding and crown cornices gave the appearance of strength, wealth, and power. The graceful columns, artwork, and statues made the diner feel he was a part of elegance of another era. One could imagine himself the guest of a Roman emperor, an Egyptian pharaoh, or an English king. A sense of security abounded when entering the dining hall. There was the anticipation that a spectacular dining event was about to reveal itself.

Having been a guest multiple times on Cunard Line's *Queen Elizabeth II*, in the 1990s, I enjoyed that feeling of luxury when entering their Britannia Restaurant. It gave one the expectation that a great occasion was imminent. Live classical music was heard at the entrance of the restaurant. It could have been a quartet of violins or a single harp. A meal fit for a king was expected, and then pleasantly experienced. The spectacular dining promised by the initial ambiance soon came to fruition.

Each table was dressed in a fine tablecloth, elegant silverware, and sparkling crystal. At least two waiters were assigned to each table. Food orders were taken, and the aroma-emitting dishes were always promptly delivered to the correct recipient. The waitstaff always knew the name of each guest and respectfully greeted him. An additional junior waiter was always within sight and available in the event a guest wanted or needed something extra. Nothing was ever late, and the waiters constantly behaved in a professional and polite manner. The dining experience was the epitome of luxury.

On *Dark Ship*, dining was a bitter disappointment. The experience of food satisfaction was not commensurate with the promise of the elegance visually assured upon entry. I had a memorable steak that would have given the leather sole on my shoe competition for toughness. At every seating, there was at least one order that was placed in front of the wrong diner. If a guest requested a condiment, it often came so late, the diner had already finished his meal. Coffee was almost never served with the dessert; it was habitually late. Many diners prefer to have coffee and dessert served together. When they requested that, the waiters acted like they were being asked for an item of great difficulty. Hence, proper service was always lacking on *Dark Ship*. Confusion and dissatisfaction abounded in the dining room. There were occasions when we had finished our appetizers, and while waiting for our main course, the table next to us was being served their dessert.

One incident occurred in the dining room when I ordered an item from the menu that was accompanied with broccoli rabe.

When the order was delivered to me, it did not contain broccoli rabe. I called the waiter and asked if he could deliver me the missing vegetable. He, looking puzzled, told me it was on my plate. I scrutinized my plate and looked back to my waiter and, thinking there was a language problem, indicated I would like broccoli rabe. Again, looking puzzled, he pointed to my plate and told me it was right there. I told him the vegetable he was pointing at was broccoli, not broccoli rabe. Again he told me that it was broccoli rabe. Realizing there may have been a communication problem due to language, I asked that he send the head waiter over.

The head waiter arrived in about thirty minutes, when we were all finished eating, asking what the problem was. I told him I didn't get any broccoli rabe. Just like the waiter, he told me I did receive broccoli rabe. Again, we traded our beliefs until he told me that broccoli and broccoli rabe were the same vegetable. I explained that I was half Italian and had been eating broccoli and broccoli rabe all my life, and they are two different vegetables. He indicated that on this ship the broccoli I was served was the same thing as broccoli rabe. My tablemates and I were astounded. We were now convinced that the waitstaff and kitchen staff were completely uneducated in the ways of kitchen knowledge.

Ann Marie, a knowledgeable Italian-American woman from Arizona, said, "I knew it, I knew it! They also don't know what oregano or basil is. I never tasted it in their 'Italian' meals. They are a kitchen staff that has never been trained in anything that is Italian or gourmet."

I think that sums up the incompetence of the staff on the entire ship. Along with a lack of supervision, *Dark Ship's* staff is immensely undertrained.

What happened? What caused the change in dining atmosphere from then to what it has now become? Is it the changes in our values caused by time, where efficiency is no longer expected? Or is it just a financial matter where an attempt is being made to take a product and reduce its cost so the bottom line is more attractive to investors?

After much discussion of this subject with my tablemates, I believe there are several factors to be considered. At one time *Dark Ship's* cruise line was known for formal dressing. Gentlemen were always required to wear ties and a jacket in the restaurant. During formal dress nights, tuxedos for men and gowns for women were required. There were no exceptions to these dress rules. The standard has now been lowered on formality. It seems now that society's standards are lowered. The public is becoming less formal. Other cruise lines have tapped into this change and have no dress requirements. It seems that *Dark Ship's* cruise line is also recognizing this change. I notice while there still are formal nights, the non-formal evening attire has been altered where, although a jacket is still required, no longer is a tie compulsory for gentlemen in the main dining room.

Even if less formality is accepted, there is no excuse for incompetency, ineptitude, and apathy among the workers. Disrespect toward the guests should never be tolerated. It is these appalling elements that riled us aboard *Dark Ship*.

There was an area of amusement that was offered on the last leg of my world cruise: observing the one-week, transatlantic passengers as they exited the dining room. There was a serving table that contained several after-dinner items. These included sugared ginger, chocolate mints, toothpicks, and small sweets. We found great humor in viewing these departing guests look over their shoulder to see if anyone was watching, and when they felt safe, they would fill their pockets with the items on the dishes. It was always fun to see if we could guess which passenger was a prospective thief. We then guessed if he was to be a greedy or just a moderate thief. I always wondered why someone would place a few dollars' worth of an item like chocolate or sticky, sugared ginger into the pocket of an expensive tuxedo. The women thieves were of lesser numbers than the men. They often had expensive purses that were in jeopardy of being forever damaged by melted chocolate.

Mindy posed the question to those of us seated at the table, "Why would someone who paid tens of thousands of dollars for a luxury cruise act like a lowlife thief?"

Bill responded, "Maybe it's an act of revenge because they feel like they were nickel and dimed to death for everything on this cruise." Bob said he just reported everything that dissatisfied him to the purser or the head chef. He thought that was the assurance he desired to right the wrongs on this ship.

Ann Marie asked, "What about you, Al? What do you feel is the best way to rectify the many problems we endured?"

I replied, "I think I'll write a book and call it *Dark Ship*."

www.ingramcontent.com/pod-product-compliance
Lightning Source LLC
Chambersburg PA
CBHW050928260726
48660CB00001B/452